The Story of

WORLD W

IRENA SENDLER

by **Marcia Vaughan**

with illustrations by **Ron Mazellan**

Additional material by **Michele Simms-Burton**

Lee & Low Books Inc.
New York

For Brigitte Schran Brown, dear friend and expert translator.
For my "spysters," Susan Pearson, Darrin Jayne, and
Linda Fortune. And for Mr. History, Kyle Crews. — M.V.

For my students at IWU—be strong and always courageous.
— R.M.

This story is true to the facts of Irena Sendler's life and the times during which she lived. It is a narrative biography in which some imagined scenes, people, thoughts, and dialogue have been included. These parts of the story are dramatic extensions of historically documented events and interactions. The author thanks Severin Hochberg, historian formerly at the Center for Advanced Holocaust Studies at the United States Holocaust Memorial Museum for seventeen years and currently teaching history at the University of Maryland-Baltimore County, for reviewing this story and for his valuable input.

The editor thanks Ksenia Winnicki for her help with the pronunciations.

Text from *Irena's Jars of Secrets* copyright © 2011 by Marcia Vaughan

Illustrations from *Irena's Jars of Secrets* copyright © 2011 by Ron Mazellan

Sidebar text by Michele Simms-Burton copyright © 2018 by Lee & Low Books Inc.

Photo credits: p. 7 "The typhus louse shaking hands with Death. Colour lithograph" by O. Grin. Courtesy of the Wellcome Collection, London, United Kingdom. Used under a Creative Commons License 4.0. https://wellcomecollection.org/works/vzyuffya • p. 9 Everett Historical / Shutterstock. com • p. 10 Map by Charice Silverman © Lee & Low Books, 2018 • p. 17 United States Holocaust Memorial Museum, courtesy of National Archives and Records Administration, College Park • p. 22 R Scapinello / Shutterstock.com • p. 30 United States Holocaust Memorial Museum, courtesy of Zydowski Instytut Historyczny • p. 36 World History Archive / Alamy Stock Photo • p. 37 United States Holocaust Memorial Museum, courtesy of National Archives and Records Administration, College Park • p. 43 Photo by Mariusz Kubik, http://www.mariuszkubik.pl - own work, http://commons.wikimedia.org/wiki/User:Kmarius, used under a Creative Commons Attribution 3.0 unported license, https://commons.wikimedia.org/w/index.php?curid=2897853

The views or opinions expressed in this book, and the context in which the images are used, do not necessarily reflect the views or policy of, nor imply approval or endorsement by, the United States Holocaust Memorial Museum.

LEE & LOW BOOKS Inc., 95 Madison Avenue, New York, NY 10016
leeandlow.com

Edited by Louise May and Cheryl Klein

Book design by Charice Silverman

Book production by The Kids at Our House

Manufactured in the United States of America by Lake Book Manufacturing, Inc.

The text is set in Volkhorn.

The display font is set in Avenir.

The illustrations are rendered in oil on canvas and enhanced in Photoshop for this edition.

10 9 8 7 6 5 4 3 2 1

First Edition

Cataloging-in-Publication data is on file with the Library of Congress.

ISBN 978-1-62014-791-7

TABLE OF CONTENTS

CHAPTER 1
A DAUGHTER'S PROMISE

On a cold February day in 1910, a baby girl was born to a Catholic family in a small town near **Warsaw,** Poland. Her parents named their daughter Irena and raised her to respect all people, regardless of their religion or race.

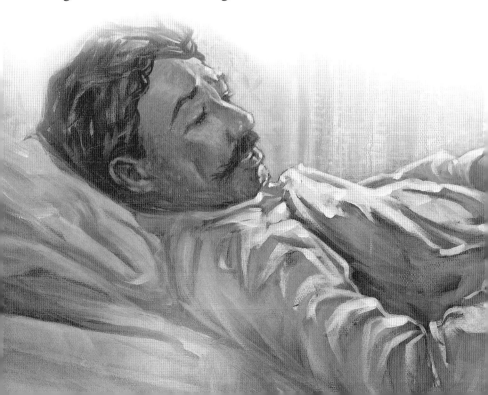

When Irena was seven years old, a **typhus epidemic** broke out in Warsaw. Irena's father was the only doctor in the area who would treat poor Jewish patients, but soon he too came down with the disease. As he lay dying, he held his daughter's hand and told her that if she ever saw someone drowning, she must jump in and try to save that person, even if she could not swim.

Irena never forgot her father's words and his dedication to helping those in need.

Typhus

Typhus is an **infectious** disease caused by bacteria that travel with body lice, chiggers, or fleas. From January 1917 to July 1918, typhus swept through Warsaw. **World War I** had created shortages of food and medical care throughout Europe. When former prisoners of war returned home to Poland, they carried lice with them. The lack of proper nutrition, medical attendants and supplies, and even soap and clean water made it difficult to fight the resulting epidemic.

Many Jewish people in Warsaw experienced **anti-Semitism** that forced them to live in crowded conditions. Because of this population **density**, typhus spread among Jews at a higher rate than other groups. Some anti-Semites used this circumstance to justify harassing or **segregating** Jews—a prejudice that affected the treatment of Jewish people in Poland for years to come.

To end the 1918 epidemic, authorities disinfected and cleaned many homes in Warsaw. They also set up delousing stations to kill the lice. At these stations, people were given hot water, soap, and **kerosene** oil and ordered to bathe. Their clothes and belongings were placed on a train, which was then sealed in a tunnel and sprayed with steam and poisonous gas. Afterward, anyone who arrived on the train could board it again and continue their journey. These efforts helped to get rid of the lice that carried typhus. Nevertheless, between 24,000 and 25,000 people died of typhus in Warsaw between 1917 and 1918.

This 1919 poster from Russia shows a typhus louse shaking hands with a skeleton that represents Death. The Russian text reads, "The louse and death are friends and comrades. Kill all lice carrying infection!"

Germany after World War I

After Germany surrendered in World War I, leaders from twenty-seven countries **negotiated** what became known as the **Treaty of Versailles**. Under Article 231 of the treaty, commonly known as the "War Guilt Clause," Germany and its **allies** were forced to accept full responsibility for the war. The treaty also required Germany to pay **reparations** for the damage the war had caused—a sum eventually set at 132 billion gold marks, or more than $400 billion today. Finally, it redrew Germany's boundaries with eight other countries, resulting in the loss of 25,000 miles of German land.

Many Germans felt humiliated by the terms of the treaty, which had been settled without their participation. World War I had ruined the German banking system and **infrastructure**, so it was difficult for the government to pay the reparations, even after the sum was reduced. German money lost much of its value, and the country experienced a **recession.** This compounded Germany's sense of defeat and failure.

Adolf Hitler scorned the enormous reparations that Germany had to pay under the treaty. He and the

Adolf Hitler in 1933, wearing an armband with a swastika, the symbol of the Nazis.

members of his National Socialist German Workers' Party—better known as **Nazis**—used the struggling economy and the national sense of humiliation to rally people to their cause. Hitler became **chancellor** of Germany in 1933, and the "Führer," or leader, in 1934. He convinced the citizens that to make Germany great again, the country would need to expand. The Nazis set their sights on their eastern neighbor: Poland.

Europe, September 1939

Land under full German control in February 1936.

This region remained part of Germany after the Treaty of Versailles, but the treaty forbade the country from keeping military troops there. Hitler moved soldiers into the area in March 1936.

Nazis took charge of the government of Austria and united it with Germany in March 1938.

Germany took over this largely German-speaking region of Czechoslovakia, known as the Sudetenland, in October 1938.

Germany invaded and began controlling the majority of Czechoslovakia in March 1939.

In August 1939, Germany and the Soviet Union made a secret pact that allowed Germany to invade and conquer this half of Poland beginning on September 1, 1939.

The Soviet Union claimed the rest of Poland by the end of the month.

CHAPTER TWO

OCCUPATION

In 1939 Adolf Hitler's German army invaded Poland. This was the start of **World War II**. Hitler intended to control all of Europe under German rule and **eliminate** the races, minorities, and other groups that he believed were **inferior** to the Germans. At the top of Hitler's list were the Jews, whom he saw as enemies of Germany and partly to blame for the country's defeat in World War I.

Nearly four hundred thousand Jews lived in the Warsaw area. Late in 1940 German soldiers forced these Jews into the Warsaw **Ghetto**, a neighborhood of run-down apartment buildings that was sealed off by a high brick wall. The German occupying forces took their homes, their money, and their belongings. Trapped inside, the people awaited their fate at the hands of those who had imprisoned them.

Irena Sendler was twenty-nine years old when the war began, and a senior administrator in the Warsaw Social Welfare Department. She remembered her father's words from many years ago. *The Jewish people are drowning*, she thought, and she knew in her heart that she had to help them.

One day Irena approached a ghetto entrance.

"Halt!" snapped the guard, raising his rifle. "No one is allowed in or out of the ghetto."

Irena, wearing the uniform of a nurse, held out papers from the epidemic control department. "I

have permission to enter to **investigate** an **outbreak** of typhus," she said.

Entering the ghetto was like entering a nightmare. The people inside were struggling to survive. They did not have enough food, water, medicine, or heating fuel.

Irena's heart filled with grief. As she walked through the ghetto, hungry children cried out. People lay sick and starving in the streets. Everywhere Irena turned, she saw death and despair.

For the next two years Irena went to the ghetto often. Defying German orders, she and her coworkers registered Jewish families under Christian names so they could receive aid. *The food, clothes, and medicine I* **smuggle** *in are not enough*, she thought bitterly. Everyone was suffering, especially the children. Irena felt she must do more.

The Warsaw Ghetto

When German troops invaded Poland in September 1939, one-third of Warsaw's population was Jewish. German troops forced this population and Jews from surrounding areas—an estimated 400,000 people—to move into a section of the city less than a mile and a half in area, surrounded by ten-foot walls topped with barbed wire. Eventually, this segregated section became known as the Warsaw Ghetto.

Not only did this type of segregation humiliate many Jews who viewed themselves as Polish citizens, it also made it difficult for them to conduct their daily affairs. To leave the ghetto, Jews had to get official permission from the military and cross through a checkpoint to the rest of the city. Living conditions were overcrowded and **unsanitary**, so illness spread quickly. The Nazis limited the amount of food and heating fuel allowed in the ghetto, and tens of thousands of people died of hunger or cold.

Many Jews did not accept these **inhumane** conditions. They also became aware that Nazis were sending

Jews to **concentration** and **extermination camps**. In the summer of 1942, about 300,000 people were deported from Warsaw to a newly built camp at **Treblinka**. While Jewish resistance groups were already fighting back, this mass deportation inspired them to greater action.

On January 18, 1943, a group of Jewish fighters interrupted a deportation operation, confusing the German soldiers enough to allow some deportees to escape. Most of the Jewish people remaining in the ghetto went into hiding. When the Germans tried to resume deportations on April 19, a group of Jewish fighters rose up and forced the soldiers to retreat outside the ghetto wall. The struggle continued for another month, as the Germans **razed** the buildings in the ghetto to wipe out the fighters' hiding places. By the time the revolt ended on May 16, 56,000 Jews had been captured, 7,000 were killed, and another 7,000 were deported to Treblinka. This revolt is known as the Warsaw Ghetto Uprising.

While Warsaw had the largest ghetto, the Nazis established ghettos in cities throughout Europe,

FROM LEFT TO RIGHT: **Hanka Lamet; her mother, Matylda Lamet Goldfinger; Chana Zeilinwarger; Leo Kartuzinsky; and an unidentified boy are forced out of hiding during the Warsaw Ghetto Uprising, May 1943.**

including Kraków, Lodz, and Bialystok, Poland; Lwów in the Ukraine; Minsk in Belarus; and Vilna (Vilnius) and Kovno (Kaunas) in Lithuania. It is estimated that more than 900,000 Jews dwelled in ghettos at some point before or during World War II.

CHAPTER THREE
IRENA THE SMUGGLER

In 1942 the Nazis began sending Jews to Treblinka, an extermination camp about sixty miles from Warsaw. In a race to save as many children as possible, Irena joined **Zegota**, a secret organization that was helping Jews in Poland survive and find places of safety. Using the code name Jolanta and a pass from the **Contagious** Disease Department, Irena gained entry into the ghetto to check sanitary conditions. This gave her and her network of **social workers** and rescuers a chance to sneak in food, medicine, and money.

Irena became head of the children's department and, along with other Zegota members, came up with clever ways to smuggle children out of the ghetto. But first she had to convince Jewish parents to let their children be taken away and placed with non-Jewish families or organizations outside the ghetto.

Like most families, the Wolmans did not want to give up their child.

"Is it better for Elka to suffer and starve behind these walls?" Irena asked. "And what will happen when the soldiers come to send you to the camp at Treblinka?"

"The Nazis say no harm will come to us there," Mr. Wolman argued.

"That's a lie," Irena told him. "The people who go there are killed."

Mrs. Wolman's face was wet with tears. "If we give you our daughter, can you promise us she'll live?"

"No," Irena said. "But if she stays here, she will surely die."

"How will we get back together when the war is over?" Mr. Wolman asked.

"If she stays here, she will surely die."

"I'll keep your child's real name and new identity on a secret list so you can find her," Irena promised the worried parents.

Suddenly the door downstairs slammed open, and the sound of soldiers' boots pounding on the front steps echoed upstairs.

"They're coming!" Mrs. Wolman cried. "Take her!"

The Wolmans quickly kissed Elka good-bye. The child cried out as Irena took Elka from her mother's arms and hurried away through the hall and down the back stairway.

Concentration and Extermination Camps

The Nazis believed in a system of hateful and racist ideas that proclaimed the superiority of white people, or "Aryans," over all others. Using this system, they sent "undesirable" people to two different kinds of camps.

The Nazis first set up concentration camps in 1933 to lock up criminals and political **dissidents.** Initially, concentration camps functioned very much like prisons, simply detaining people in harsh conditions. But as Germany expanded the camp system, prisoners

The words "Arbeit Macht Frei" on the gate at Auschwitz, the largest concentration camp, lied to incoming prisoners: "Work sets you free."

in the camps became forced laborers as well, building camp facilities, working in factories, or mining raw materials. Many died of overwork, sickness, cold, or hunger. More and more people were also sent to the camps based solely upon their identity, including Roma people, gays and lesbians, people of African descent, and especially Jews. After Germany invaded Poland in 1939, the Nazis began to kill prisoners in the concentration camps directly, particularly when they could no longer work.

Extermination camps were established specifically to carry out the Nazis' "Final Solution": the complete **annihilation** of the Jewish people. Beginning in 1941, the Nazis transported Jews from all over Europe to six camps scattered throughout occupied Poland, where they were killed using poison gas. This kind of deliberate destruction of one specific group of people is known as a *genocide*. It is estimated that a total of eighteen million prisoners—about six million of them Jewish—died in Nazi concentration and extermination camps due to hunger, illness, physical exhaustion, insufficient living conditions, or organized mass murder. This **systematic** killing by the Nazis and their allies is known as the **Holocaust**.

CHAPTER FOUR

ESCAPE FROM THE GHETTO

One day Irena and another Zegota member hid a baby under the floorboards of the ambulance they were driving out of the ghetto. Riding between them was a dog.

"I see you come here two, sometimes three times a day," a guard at the gate said to Irena. "I want to see what you've got in there."

At that moment the child whimpered, and Irena's heart froze. If the guard found the baby, they would all be shot. So Irena hit the dog on its paw. Immediately the dog began to bark, drowning out the child's sounds.

"Shut that dog up before I put a bullet in it!" snapped the guard, and he waved them through the gate.

As they drove away, Irena patted the dog's head. Their secret passenger had been saved.

Older children who were being rescued understood the need for silence, secrecy, and **deception**.

"Rivka," Irena said, "if you can pretend to be very ill,

"We would go to the ghetto and try to get as many children as possible because the situation would worsen every day."

–Irena Sendler

25

we'll take you out in the ambulance; and we'll hide your little brother, Aaron, under your stretcher." Then Irena warned Aaron that no matter what happened, he must not make a sound.

At the exit gate a guard threw open the door of the ambulance.

"This girl does not look sick to me," he shouted, jabbing her with his rifle.

Instead of crying in pain, Rivka moaned as if she were very ill. But the terror was too much for Aaron. He began to sob. To cover the sound, Rivka began coughing.

"Don't get too close unless you want to catch typhus," the ambulance driver warned.

"Typhus?" The guard backed away. "Get her out of here at once!"

On other trips into the ghetto, Irena and her Zegota team carried babies and young children out in baskets, boxes, tool chests, sacks, and suitcases. When garbage was removed from the ghetto, children were sometimes hidden on the truck under piles of trash. Escapes with older children were made through the sewers or old courthouse, or by **bribing** the guards to let them escape.

Once the children were out of the ghetto they were given new identity papers and taken to live in orphanages, **convents,** or non-Jewish foster homes. It was not easy to find families who were willing to pretend that a Jewish child was one of their own. Yet people did come forward, ready to help save the lives of innocent children. Irena and her Zegota workers told the foster families

and organizations that the Jewish children they agreed to care for must be reunited with their parents or relatives when the war ended.

As she had promised, Irena kept careful records of each child's Jewish name and false identity on two identical lists. She placed the lists in jars, which were buried under an apple tree in a friend's garden across the street from the German soldiers' barracks. As more children were rescued, Irena dug up the jars, added their names to the lists, and buried the jars again.

Zegota

The nickname "Zegota" was short for the "Konrad Zegota Committee," even though no man named Konrad Zegota ever existed. That kind of deception was typical of Zegota, formally known as the Polish Council to Aid Jews. Based in Warsaw, it **coordinated** the efforts of various individuals and groups to help Poland's Jewish population during World War II. Jewish, Christian, governmental, and political organizations all participated in its activities.

Over one hundred Zegota **cells** operated throughout Poland, especially in Warsaw and other major cities. Members found hiding places for Jews in both urban and rural areas. Maurycy Herling-Grudzinski, a rich Jewish lawyer who was able to pass as a Christian, hid between five and six hundred people on his estate outside Warsaw. Zegota then provided a small amount of money each month to help those in hiding survive. One cell created false papers, like birth certificates and identity cards, to allow Jews to travel safely through the German-patrolled streets. The organization also

Zegota used this photograph to create a false identification card for one of its volunteers, Izabela Biezunska. Note the "official" stamps on the corners.

transmitted messages from Jewish leaders to the outside world.

Zegota worked out of six secret apartments, with an unofficial headquarters at 24 Zurawia Street in Warsaw. There members could find out about future meetings, get supplies of food and clothing, and make arrangements for documents or housing for Jews in hiding. There were also many "branch offices," like the small grocery store run by an old woman everyone called "Babcia," or "Granny." Granny stashed papers, money, and illegal books in hiding places around the store, and frequently tucked Jewish children fleeing the police under sacks of potatoes or other supplies.

The German authorities offered cash rewards for revealing the location of Jewish people in hiding, and concealing a Jew was a crime punishable by death. Zegota and the Jewish people they served thus struggled against the constant threat of *blackmail*, where someone would demand money in return for keeping a secret. One of Zegota's leaders was quoted as saying, "To help a Jew could cost you your life, so for the same life, you might as well help several Jews."

While exact numbers are impossible to come by, it is estimated that Zegota helped at least 4,000 Jewish people with housing, food, false documents, or medical care.

CHAPTER FIVE
BETRAYED

I n October 1943 Irena was **betrayed** to the Germans. They were told that she was smuggling children out of the ghetto. Irena was arrested by the **Gestapo,** the German secret police, and taken to **Pawiak** prison.

One day a Gestapo officer entered Irena's cell. "You tell us the whereabouts of every child you helped escape and the names of your **collaborators**," he demanded, "or you will die."

If Irena told the Germans the location of the buried jars, she knew that the children, the people who sheltered them, and those who assisted her would all be killed. Over the next three months the police beat and **tortured** her, but Irena kept her silence.

And so she was sentenced to death.

As Irena awaited **execution**, she felt

strangely at peace. Although she would die, she knew many others would live.

The day after Irena was to be killed, posters that hung all over Warsaw listed Irena Sendler among the people who had been shot by a **firing squad**. The Gestapo did not know that at the last moment members of Zegota had paid a bribe. Instead of being shot, Irena had secretly been set free.

When the Gestapo later learned of the deception, they sent search parties to look for Irena. But like the children she helped rescue, Irena went into hiding. Using a new identity, she  continued to work with Zegota from her hiding places. The Gestapo never found her.

The Gestapo

The Gestapo served as the official secret police of Nazi Germany. The nickname "Gestapo" was adapted from the full German name Ge*heime* Sta*ats* Po*lizei*. The organization emerged from a state-level secret police group established in 1933, which was then combined with other German security forces over the next few years. It was declared a national police force in 1936.

Gestapo officers arrested, jailed, and tortured anyone who did not agree with the Nazi Party. They particularly monitored the activities of **Communists**, churches, and student groups, who often stood up to Nazi beliefs. A 1936 law gave the Gestapo freedom from review or punishment by any court, and officers became known for their brutality and cruelty. They encouraged the German people to spy on each other and report any **rebellious** behavior or opinions. According to one historian, as many as 80 percent of all Gestapo investigations began with a report from a neighbor or family member.

Gestapo officers also played a major role in the Holocaust. They supervised the Jewish ghettos and

This tree near the entrance to Pawiak Prison holds memorial plaques for people tortured and killed there by the Gestapo.

purposefully created the inhumane conditions that led to hundreds of thousands of deaths. A division of the Gestapo under **Adolf Eichmann** was responsible for transporting millions of people to the concentration camps, while Gestapo task forces, or *Einsatzgruppen*, killed thousands of Jews in the Soviet Union.

After World War II ended, the **Allies** held an international military **tribunal** in the German city of Nuremberg, at which twenty-one major Nazi leaders and six groups, including the Gestapo, were tried for war crimes. This trial revealed much of the information known today about the Nazis and the Holocaust. The

Gestapo was convicted of war crimes as a group, but few of its leaders or members were ever individually charged. One notable exception was Eichmann, who was captured in Argentina in 1960 and later tried and executed in Israel.

A Gestapo officer is put on trial at Nuremberg in December 1945.

CHAPTER SIX
IRENA'S JARS

After World War II ended in 1945, Irena returned once again to the apple tree. She dug down through the dirt and rocks in the garden and uncovered the jars and their precious contents. Irena counted the names. On her lists were about twenty-five hundred Jewish children who had been rescued, though the exact number is not known.

Irena gave the lists to the Jewish National Committee, a group of organizations that helped Jews in Poland during and after World War II. The committee found that most of the children had survived the war. But Irena's hopes of re-uniting them with their families faded as she learned that nearly all of the parents had died in extermination camps. Using the information in Irena's lists, the committee found living relatives for some children. Other children stayed with their non-Jewish families, and some children went to live in other countries.

For many years Poland's Communist government ignored Irena's story and the stories of other brave Polish people who helped Jews during the war. But Irena's selfless deeds were recognized in 1965 by Yad Vashem, the Jewish people's memorial to the Holocaust. Irena Sendler was honored as "Righteous Among the Nations," a title given to non-Jews who risked their own lives to save Jewish people during the Holocaust. In 1991 she was made an honorary citizen of Israel.

After the fall of Poland's Communist government, Irena was awarded the Order of the White Eagle, Poland's highest honor. She was also given the Jan Karski Freedom Award for Valor and Compassion by Freedom House and the American Center of Polish Culture. And in 2007 she was nominated for the Nobel Peace Prize. When her photograph appeared in the newspapers, people began to call. "I remember your face," the callers said. "It was you who took me out of the ghetto."

Irena Sendler spent the last years of her life in a nursing home in Warsaw. She was cared for by **Elzbieta Ficowska,** who as a baby had been smuggled out of the ghetto in a carpenter's box hidden under a load of bricks.

In 2008, at the age of ninety-eight, Irena Sendler was one of the last surviving members of the children's department of Zegota. Although she passed away on May 12 of that year, her story of caring and courage lives on.

Irena Sendler never thought of herself as a hero. She only did what she felt she must, and wished she could have done more.

"Every child saved with my help and the help of all the wonderful secret messengers, who today are no longer living, is the justification of my existence on this earth, and not a title to glory."

–Irena Sendler

Elzbieta Ficowska

Elzbieta Ficowska was five or six months old when her parents handed her to Stanislawa Bussold, a midwife for Jewish women in the Warsaw Ghetto. Stanislawa raised her as her own daughter, and Elzbieta did not know that Stanislawa was her adopted mother until she was seventeen years old.

When Elzbieta began searching for the truth about her life, she discovered that her parents died in the camps. But she met people who knew them, and thus learned about her parents, other family members, and the lives they led before World War II. This helped her to better understand her family, their choice to give her up, and the history that she survived.

In reflecting on her quest to learn about her past, Elzbieta stated: "I did not want to be disloyal towards my mother [Stanislawa], cause her pain. I simply put that information out of my mind, and for many years we did not talk about it. When my own daughter was six months old, I understood what separation with her child must have meant to my mother. I suddenly grasped it. And I started searching for traces of my

Irena Sendler (with headband) in 2008 with some of the people she rescued, including Elzbieta Ficowska (standing in glasses).

Jewish family. Both of my dead mothers are with me and shall stay with me to the end. Their presence reminds me that there is nothing more devastating than hatred and nothing more precious than human kindness."

To read her reflections in full, visit http://moirodzice. org.pl/en_elzbieta_ficowska.php.

TIMELINE

1910 February 15: Irena Krzyzanowska is born in Warsaw, Poland. She grows up in the nearby town of Otwock.

1914 June 28: World War I begins when Archduke Franz Ferdinand is assassinated in Sarajevo, Bosnia.

1917 February: Irena's father, Dr. Stanislaw Krzyzanowski, dies during a typhus epidemic.

1918 November 11: Germany signs an agreement ending World War I.

1919 June 28: the Treaty of Versailles is signed.

1931 Irena marries Mieczyslaw Sendler.

1933 January 30: Adolf Hitler is named chancellor of Germany and begins to consolidate power.

1939 September 1: Hitler's army invades Poland, and World War II begins.

1940 Irena and a small team of fellow volunteers begin assisting the Jewish community in Warsaw. Jews living in the Warsaw area are forced into the Warsaw Ghetto.

1942 July: The Nazis begin sending Jews to the Treblinka extermination camp.

October: Zegota is founded.

1943 January 18: Jewish fighters interrupt a deportation from the Warsaw Ghetto to Treblinka, and deportations are temporarily suspended.

April 19: The Nazis attempt to resume deportations, and the Warsaw Ghetto Uprising begins.

May 16: The Uprising comes to an end.

August-September: Irena and her team join Zegota.

October 19: Irena is betrayed to the Germans and taken to Pawiak prison.

1944 January 20: Irena is freed and goes into hiding.

1945 World War II ends in Europe when Germany surrenders.

1947 Irena divorces Mieczyslaw Sendler and marries Stefan Zgrzembski. They eventually have two children.

1948 Irena is brutally interrogated by the Polish Communist secret police.

1965 Irena is named a "Righteous Among the Nations" by Yad Vashem, the Jewish people's memorial to the Holocaust. The Communist government of Poland refuses to allow her to travel to Israel to accept the recognition.

1983 Irena is finally able to visit Israel and be recognized as "Righteous Among the Nations."

1989 Poland's Communist government is disbanded.

1991 Irena is made an honorary citizen of Israel.

1999 Students at a high school in Uniontown, Kansas, write and stage a play about Irena entitled *Life in a Jar*. It is eventually produced over 200 times, bringing significant public attention to Irena's heroism.

2003 Irena is awarded the Order of the White Eagle, Poland's highest honor, and the Jan Karski Freedom Award for Valor and Compassion by Freedom House and the American Center of Polish Culture.

2008 May 12: Irena dies at the age of ninety-eight.

Adolf Eichmann (AD-olf IKE-mann) *person* Gestapo officer who organized the transportation of Jewish people and other "undesirables" to the concentration and extermination camps

Adolf Hitler (AD-olf HIT-ler) *person* leader of the National Socialist German Workers' Party (Nazi Party); Chancellor of Germany from 1933 to 1945

Allies (AL-eyes) *proper noun* the nations that fought Germany, Italy, and Japan in World War II, including the United States, the Soviet Union, the United Kingdom, and China as well as many others

allies (AL-eyes) *noun* people, groups, or countries that gives aid and/or support to another

annihilation (uh-NY-uh-lay-SHUN) *noun* total destruction

anti-Semitism (AN-tee seh-muh-teh-ZUM) *noun* a race-based dislike of or discrimination against Jewish people as a group; a person who demonstrates anti-Semitism is an anti-Semite

betray (BEE-tray) *verb* to help the enemy of a person, group, or country

bribe (BRYB) *noun* something of value that is given to get someone to do something; *verb* to pay someone a bribe

cell (SELL) *noun* a smaller, self-contained unit of a larger organization

chancellor (CHAN-suh-lore) *noun* the chief nonroyal leader of some European countries

collaborators (KO-lab-or-ATE-tors) *noun* people who work together in order to accomplish something

Communist (KOM-yew-nist) *proper noun* person who believes in Communism, a social and political system in which most property is owned and shared by all people in a country

concentration camp (KON-son-tray-shun KAMP) *noun* place where prisoners or refugees are held

contagious (kon-TAY-jus) *adjective* capable of being spread from one person to another

convent (KON-vent) *noun* building where a group of people devoted to religious life live, often Catholic nuns

coordinate (koh-ORE-din-ate) *verb* to help things or people work together smoothly

deception (DEE-sep-shun) *noun* the act of making someone believe what is not true

density (DEN-suh-tee) *noun* a state in which all of the parts of a thing are packed closely together

dissident (DIS-ee-dint) *noun* a person who disagrees with (dissents from) another opinion or group

eliminate (EE-lim-en-ate) *noun* to get rid of something

Elzbieta Ficowska (ELZH-bee-ay-tuh FEE-sohv-skuh) *person* a woman who was rescued from the Warsaw Ghetto by Irena Sendler

epidemic (eh-puh-DEH-mik) *noun* outbreak of disease that spreads very quickly and affects a large number of people

execution (EK-see-CUE-shun) *noun* to kill someone as penalty for committing a crime

extermination camp (ek-STUR-muh-nay-shun kamp) *noun* place where large numbers of people are sent to be killed

firing squad (FYER-ing skwahd) *noun* group of soldiers assigned to shoot a prisoner who has been sentenced to death

Gestapo (geh-STAH-poh) *proper noun* official secret police force of Nazi Germany known for its brutal methods

ghetto (GET-oh) *noun* poor, run-down part of a city where people of the same race, religion, or ethnic background live

Holocaust (HOH-luh-kost) *proper noun* the systematic killing of millions of Jews and other minorities and groups in Europe by the Germans and their allies during World War II

infectious (en-FEK-shus) *adjective* able to be spread easily, especially by infection

inferior (en-FEER-ee-ore) *adjective* low in position or value

infrastructure (EN-fruh-STRUK-sure) *noun* the roads, bridges, utilities, equipment, and other common goods that allow a country or organization to function

inhumane (en-HEW-mane) *adjective* without kindness or humanity

investigate (en-VES-tee-gate) *verb* to find out the facts about something that happened

Irena Sendler (EE-ren-uh SEND-ler) *person* Polish Catholic social worker who helped rescue about 2,500 Jewish children during World War II

kerosene (KARE-oh-seen) *noun* a kind of oil used as a fuel or cleaning fluid

Nazi (NOT-see *or* NAT-see) *proper noun* member of the National Socialist German Workers' Party, which ruled Germany from 1933 to 1945; Nazis believed in German racial superiority and attempted to rid the world of people they considered enemies or undesirable

negotiate (nee-GO-shee-ate) *verb* to come to an agreement through discussion

outbreak (OUT-brake) *noun* a sudden event involving disease or fighting

Pawiak (PAH-vee-ahk) *proper noun* prison in Warsaw, Poland, used by the Gestapo during World War II to hold and torture prisoners

raze (RAYZ) *verb* to knock down or wipe something out completely

rebellious (ree-BELL-ee-us) *adjective* participating in a fight against authority

recession (ree-SEH-shun) *noun* a state in which a country's economy slows down and people suffer financial difficulties

reparations (rep-uh-RAY-shuns) *noun* money paid to another to make up for or repair some wrong

segregate (seg-ree-GATE) *verb* to separate people of different groups, particularly based on race

smuggle (SMUG-ull) *verb* to move someone or something across a border illegally

social worker (SOH-shull WUR-kur) *noun* person who works helping others with problems related to health, housing, poverty, unemployment, disabilities, and other social issues

swastika (SWAS-tee-kuh) *noun* an ancient design of an X with its legs bent at right angles, adopted by the Nazis as their official symbol

systematic (SIS-tuh-MA-tik) *adjective* organized within a system or method

torture (TOR-chur) *verb* to cause someone pain as a form of punishment or in order to force them to confess something

Treaty of Versailles (TREE-tee uv VAIR-sy) *proper noun* the peace treaty that formally ended World War I, negotiated primarily at the French palace of Versailles outside Paris

Treblinka (TRUH-bling-kuh) *proper noun* Nazi extermination camp that existed from 1942 to 1943 near Warsaw, Poland, where about 800,000 Jews were put to death during World War II

tribunal (try-BEW-null) *noun* a court, particularly a military court

typhus (TY-fus) *noun* serious infectious disease spread by lice, chiggers, or fleas, which causes intense headache, high fever, and a dark red rash

unsanitary (un-SAN-ee-tare-ee) *adjective* unhealthy or unclean

Warsaw (WOR-saw) *proper noun* capital of Poland; during World War II, the city was occupied by German troops and subjected to systematic destruction

World War I (WURLD WOR WUN) *proper noun* war in which Great Britain, France, Russia, and the United States, among other nations, fought Germany and Austria-Hungary, waged mainly in Europe from 1914 to 1918

World War II (WURLD WOR TOO) *proper noun* war in which Germany, Italy, and Japan fought the Allies, waged mainly in Europe, Asia, the South Pacific, and North Africa from 1939 to 1945

Zegota (zhyeh-GOH-tah) *proper noun* code name for the Council for Aid to Jews; Polish non-Jewish underground organization that assisted Jewish people and found places of safety for them from 1942 to 1945 during World War II

TEXT SOURCES

Ackerman, Diane. *The Zookeeper's Wife: A War Story.* New York: W. W. Norton & Company, 2007.

Anflick, Charles. *Resistance: Teen Partisans and Resisters Who Fought Nazi Tyranny.* New York: Rosen Publishing Group, 1999.

Bülow, Louis. "Irena Sendler: An Unsung Heroine." The Holocaust: Crimes, Heroes and Villains. http://www.auschwitz.dk/Sendler.htm

Downing, David. *Toward Genocide.* World Almanac Library of the Holocaust. Milwaukee, WI: World Almanac Library, 2005.

Gessner, Peter K. "Irena Sendler: WWII Rescuer and Hero." InfoPoland, University at Buffalo. http://info-poland.buffalo.edu/classroom/sendler/index.html (site discontinued).

Haas, Gerda. *These I Do Remember: Fragments from the Holocaust.* Freeport, ME: Cumberland Press, 1982.

Harrison, John Kent, and Lawrence John Spagnola. *The Courageous Heart of Irena Sendler.* Directed by John Kent Harrison. Hallmark Hall of Fame. Released April 19, 2009. DVD, 95 min.

Hevesi, Dennis. "Irena Sendler, Lifeline to Young Jews, Is Dead at 98." *New York Times* online, May 13, 2008.

http://www.nytimes.com/2008/05/13/world/europe/13sendler.html

"Irena Sendler: 1910–2008." *Jewish Virtual Library.* http://www.jewishvirtuallibrary.org/irena-sendler

Irena Sendler: In the Name of Their Mothers. Produced and directed by Mary Skinner. PBS/KQED Public Television. San Francisco: 2B Productions. Aired May 1, 2011. Released June 7, 2011. DVD, 60 min.

Life in a Jar: The Irena Sendler Project. http://www.irenasendler.org

Life in a Jar: The Irena Sendler Project. Funded by the Milken Family Foundation and Lowell Milken Center. Fort Scott, KS, 1992. DVD.

Mieszkowska, Anna. *Die Mutter der Holocaust-Kinder.* Translated for the author of this story by Brigitte Schran Brown. Munich, Germany: Verlagsgruppe Random House, 2004.

Polonsky, Antony. "Irena Sendler: Polish social worker who saved around 2,500 Jewish children from the Nazis." *The Guardian* online, May 14, 2008. http://www.theguardian.com/world/2008/may/14/secondworldwar.poland

Rymkiewicz, Jaroslaw M. , and Nina Taylor, trans. *The Final Station: Umschlagplatz.* New York: Farrar, Straus and Giroux, 1994.

Snyder, Don. "Holocaust heroine recalled by two she saved." msnbc.com, September 24, 2008. http://worldblog.msnbc.msn.com/archive/2008/09/24/1438429.aspx (URL discontinued)

Stewart, Gail B. *Life in a Warsaw Ghetto*. San Diego: Lucent Books, 1995.

Tomaszewski, Irene, and Tecia Werbowski. "Chapter 4: The Konrad Zegota Committee." *Zegota*. Project InPosterum: Preserving the Past for the Future. http://www.projectinposterum.org/docs/zegota.htm

United States Holocaust Memorial Museum. http://www.ushmm.org

Woo, Elaine. "Irena Sendler, 1910–2008: WWII savior of young Jews." *Los Angeles Times* online, May 13, 2008. http://articles.latimes.com/2008/may/13/local/me-sendler13

Yad Vashem. "Women of Valor: Stories of Women Who Rescued Jews During the Holocaust: Irena Sendler." http://www.yadvashem.org/yv/en/exhibitions/righteous-women/sendler.asp

Zullo, Allan, and Mara Bovsun. *Survivors: True Stories of Children in the Holocaust*. New York: Scholastic Inc. , 2004.

SIDEBAR SOURCES

TYPHUS

Baumslag, Naomi. *Murderous Medicine: Nazi Doctors, Human Experimentation, and Typhus.* Westport, CT: Praeger Publishers, Greenwood Publishing Group, Inc., 2005.

Goodall, E.W. "Typhus Fever in Poland, 1916 to 1919." *Proceedings of the Royal Society of Medicine.* 13.Sect Epidemiol State Med (1920): 261–276. https://www.ncbi.nlm.nih.gov/pmc/articles/PMC2152684/

Weindling, Paul. *Epidemics and Genocide in Eastern Europe, 1890-1945.* New York: Oxford University Press, 2000.

GERMANY AFTER WORLD WAR I

Schuker, Stephen A. *American "Reparations" to Germany, 1919-33: Implications for the Third-World Debt Crisis.* Princeton Studies in International Finance, no. 61. Princeton, NJ: International Finance Section, Department of Economics, Princeton University, 1988.

Suddath, Claire. "Why Did World War I Just End?" *Time* online, October 4, 2010. http://content.time.com/time/world/article/0,8599,2023140,00.html

"Treaty of Peace with Germany (Treaty of Versailles)."
Library of Congress. http://www.loc.gov/law/help/
us-treaties/bevans/m-ust000002-0043.pdf

United States Holocaust Memorial Museum. "Treaty
of Versailles, 1919." Holocaust Encyclopedia.
https://www.ushmm.org/wlc/en/article.
php?ModuleId=10005425

THE WARSAW GHETTO

Abramson, Henry. "Warsaw Ghetto Deportations (This
Week in Jewish History) Dr. Henry Abramson."
https://youtu.be/jz4lWr_ _dF8

History.com. "1939, Germans Invade Poland."
This Day in History. http://www.history.com/
this-day-in-history/germans-invade-poland

Jewish Virtual Library. "Ghettos: List of Major Jewish
Ghettos." http://www.jewishvirtuallibrary.org/
list-of-major-jewish-ghettos

———. "The Warsaw Ghetto: Map of the Ghetto."
http://www.jewishvirtuallibrary.org/
map-of-the-warsaw-ghetto

Taylor, Alan. "World War II: The Invasion of Poland and
the Winter War." *The Atlantic*. June 26, 2011. https://
www.theatlantic.com/photo/2011/06/world-war-ii-
the-invasion-of-poland-and-the-winter-
war/100094/

A Teacher's Guide to the Holocaust. "Photos: The Warsaw Ghetto Uprising, I." https://fcit.usf.edu/holocaust/resource/gallery/G1941WGU.htm

United States Holocaust Memorial Museum. "The Invasion and Occupation of Poland." https://www.ushmm.org/learn/students/learning-materials-and-resources/poles-victims-of-the-nazi-era/the-invasion-and-occupation-of-poland

————. "Invasion of Poland, Fall 1939." Holocaust Encyclopedia. https://www.ushmm.org/wlc/en/article.php?ModuleId=10005070.in

————. "Jewish Uprisings in Ghettos and Camps, 1941–1944." Holocaust Encyclopedia. https://www.ushmm.org/wlc/en/article.php?ModuleId=10005407

CONCENTRATION AND EXTERMINATION CAMPS

Aladdin Project. "The Concentration Camps, 1933–1945." Holocaust: A Call to Conscience. http://www.projetaladin.org/holocaust/en/history-of-the-holocaust-shoah/the-killing-machine/concentration-camps.html

Kirsch, Adam. "The System." *The New Yorker.* April 6, 2015. https://www.newyorker.com/magazine/2015/04/06/the-system-books-kirsch

United States Holocaust Memorial Museum. "The Final Solution." The Holocaust: A Learning Site for Students. https://www.ushmm.org/outreach/en/article.php?ModuleId=10007704

Wachsmann, Nikolaus. *KL: A History of the Nazi Concentration Camps*. New York: Farrar, Straus and Giroux, 2015.

Yad Vashem. "Frequently Asked Questions." Shoah Resource Center. http://www.un.org/en/holocaustremembrance/docs/FAQ%20Holocaust%20EN%20Yad%20Vashem.pdf

ZEGOTA

Jewish Virtual Library. "Adam Czerniakow (1880–1942)." http://www.jewishvirtuallibrary.org/adam-czerniakow

———. "Jewish Resistance: Konrad Zegota Committee." http://www.jewishvirtuallibrary.org/the-379-egota

Kopec-Gdansk, Hans Stanislav. "Zegota: 'The Council for Aid to Polish Jews.'" Holocaust Education & Archive Research Team. http://www.holocaustresearchproject.org/revolt/zegota.html

THE GESTAPO

Gavin, Philip. "The Gestapo Is Born." The History Place. http://www.historyplace.com/worldwar2/triumph/tr-gestapo.htm

Jewish Virtual Library. "Nazi Perpetrators: The Gestapo." http://www.jewishvirtuallibrary.org/the-gestapo

McDonough, Frank. *The Gestapo: The Myth and Reality of Hitler's Secret Police*. New York: Skyhorse, 2017.

Yad Vashem. "Gestapo." http://www.yadvashem.org/odot_pdf/Microsoft%20Word%20-%206284.pdf

ELZBIETA FICOWSKA

Ficowska, Elzbieta. "Children of the Holocaust Speak." Association of Children of the Holocaust in Poland. http://www.dzieciholocaustu.org.pl/szab58.php?s=en_myionas_11.php

———. "My Jewish Parents, My Polish Parents." Association of Children of the Holocaust in Poland. http://moirodzice.org.pl/en_elzbieta_ficowska.php

RECOMMENDED FURTHER READING

Nonfiction

Bascomb, Neal. *The Nazi Hunters: How a Team of Spies and Survivors Captured the World's Most Notorious Nazi.* New York: Arthur A. Levine Books/Scholastic, 2013.

Frank, Anne. *The Diary of a Young Girl.* New York: Doubleday, 1967. Reprinted in a translation by B.M. Mooyaart. New York: Bantam, 1993.

Leyson, Leon, with Marilyn J. Harran and Elisabeth B. Leyson. *The Boy on the Wooden Box: How the Impossible Became Possible . . . on Schindler's List.* New York: Atheneum Books for Young Readers/Simon & Schuster, 2015.

Mayer, Jack. *Life in a Jar: The Irena Sendler Project.* Middlebury, VT: Long Trail Press, 2011.

Mazzeo, Tilar J. *Irena's Children: A Story of True Courage.* Young Reader's Edition adapted by Mary Cronk Farrell. New York: Margaret K. McElderry Books/Simon & Schuster, 2017.

Prins, Marcel, and Peter Henk Steenhuis. *Hidden Like Anne Frank: 14 True Stories of Survival.* Translated by Laura Watkinson. New York: Arthur A. Levine Books/Scholastic, 2014.

Roy, Jennifer. *Jars of Hope: How One Woman Helped Save 2,500 Children during the Holocaust*. Illustrated by Meg Owenson. Mankato, Minn.: Capstone, 2015.

Rubin, Susan Goldman. *Irena Sendler and the Children of the Warsaw Ghetto*. Illustrated by Bill Farnsworth. New York: Holiday House, 2011.

Fiction

Cerrito, Angela. *The Safest Lie*. New York: Holiday House, 2015.

Gleitzman, Morris. *Once*. New York: Henry Holt, 2010.

Hesse, Monica. *Girl in the Blue Coat*. New York: Little, Brown Books for Young Readers, 2017.

Lowry, Lois. *Number the Stars*. Boston: Houghton Mifflin, 1989.

Orlev, Uri. *Run, Boy, Run*. Translated by Hillel Halkin. Boston: Houghton Mifflin, 2003.

Roy, Jennifer. *Yellow Star*. New York: Marshall Cavendish, 2006.

Spinelli, Jerry. *Milkweed*. New York: Alfred A. Knopf Books for Young Readers/Random House, 2003.

Zusak, Marcus. *The Book Thief*. New York: Alfred A. Knopf Books for Young Readers/Random House, 2005.

ABOUT THE AUTHOR AND ILLUSTRATOR

MARCIA VAUGHAN has written numerous books for young readers, including the picture books *The Secret to Freedom* and *Up the Learning Tree*. She was inspired to tell Irena Sendler's story after reading her obituary in 2008 and discovering more about her through the work of Life in a Jar: The Irena Sendler Project, an organization dedicated to bringing Irena Sendler's story to the world. Vaughan lives in Tacoma, Washington.

RON MAZELLAN is the illustrator of several award-winning picture books. He is also a professor of art at Indiana Wesleyan University. Mazellan was drawn to this story by Irena Sendler's character and her multiple selfless acts of kindness and courage toward those who had little hope of survival. Mazellan lives in Marion, Indiana.